DO YOU EVER

HAVE QUESTIONS

LIKE THESE?

DO YOU EVER HAVE QUESTIONS LIKE THESE?

by

Margaret Taliaferro

A Doubleday-Galilee Original
Doubleday & Company, Inc.
Garden City, New York 1979

ISBN: 0-385-14789-9
Library of Congress Catalog Card Number 78-61448
Copyright © 1979 by Margaret Taliaferro
All Rights Reserved
Printed in the United States of America
First Edition

CONTENTS

                                          page

Is there really a god?   13

Am I important?
     Do I really matter?   21

Does god love some
    people more than others?   27

How far can god's love
                  reach?   31

How much does god know
              about me?   35

How long has god known
                    me?   39

Do I <u>have</u> to love God?	41
Is God always with me?	45
Is there anyone in the world who is good all the time?	49
Would I make God unhappy if I turned away from Him?	53
If there's a God, why does there have to be Jesus Christ? And why the Holy Spirit?	71
How did it all begin? Who made the world?	81
If God made the world, who made God?	87
Why did God make people?	91
Is there really a devil?	95

Why did God make the devil? 103

Does the Bible have a happy ending? 109

I would like to be happy and safe forever. How do I go about it? 119

What is heaven like? 127

What does God want me to do when someone is mean to me? 133

Does God want me to be kind to everyone? 139

When I know I've done something wrong, what can I do about it? 155

If God forgives me, do I have to forgive other people? 159

How should I pray? 163

Will God answer my prayers? 169

Are there some prayers that won't be answered? 175

If I pray for something and it happens, did my prayers make that thing happen? 179

What does God do if two people pray opposite prayers at the same time? 185

If I pray for a sick person

in the hospital and he gets well, did the doctor make him well or did God?   195

Are my prayers really important?   199

DO YOU EVER

HAVE QUESTIONS

LIKE THESE?

Is there really a god?

There are some people who say "There is no God." But if there's no God, no mind, and no plan behind all that we see and all that we know about our world, then we have to say that everything is by chance, and that everything just

happens to _happen_.

And if there's no plan, why does the sun always come up in the east and go down in the west, and we can set our clocks by its action? Why doesn't it sometimes get all mixed up?

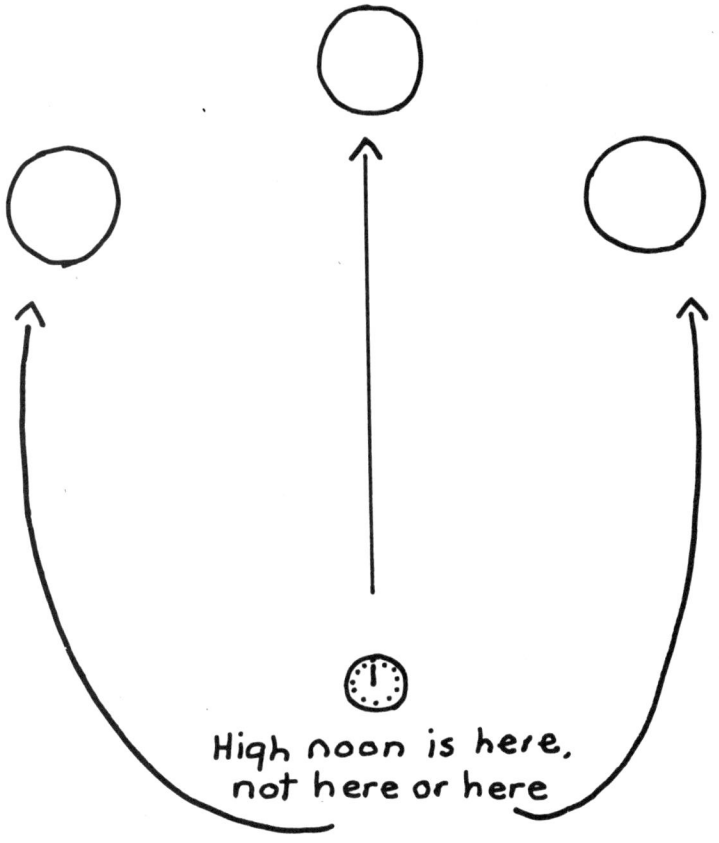

High noon is here, not here or here

And why do the tides always go out and come

in, instead of sometimes
<u>staying in</u> or <u>staying out</u>?

staying in

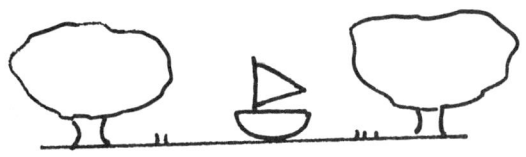

staying out

Why does winter always follow fall, and never mix

things up by getting here first?

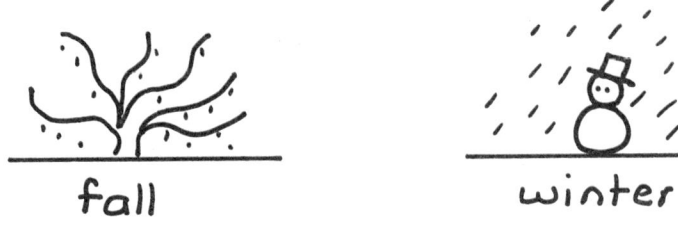

fall

winter

instead of-

winter

fall

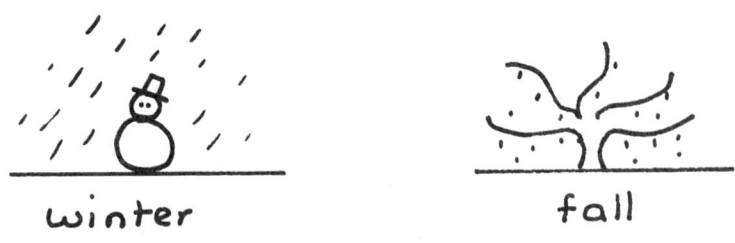

And what makes you grow? And why do you grow evenly instead of very <u>un</u>evenly?

You grow this way—

    👤 then 👤 then 👤

You don't grow this way—

    👤 or 👤 or 👤

And have you ever looked at the lines on your thumb? Well, do you know that the lines on every single thumb in all the world are <u>different</u>?

∩ ∩   ∩ ∩∩ ∩ ∩∩ ∩
thumbs with the prints
         all different.

And do you know that no one (not even the biggest brain thinking away at top speed) has been able to figure out why we stay on the ground? We have a name for this business of staying-on-the-ground, we call it gravity. But that doesn't get us very far, because we're still stuck with the question.

what is gravity?

Why don't we go flying off into space?

So it's for these — and for many, many other reasons — that there must be a God, with a plan behind all that we see here on earth.

Am I important?
Do I really matter?

Whenever you feel this way -

I'm not important, and everyone over there is very important.

or whenever you feel this way -

I'm not loved

remember that this is god's answer to you.

And, although your family loves you —

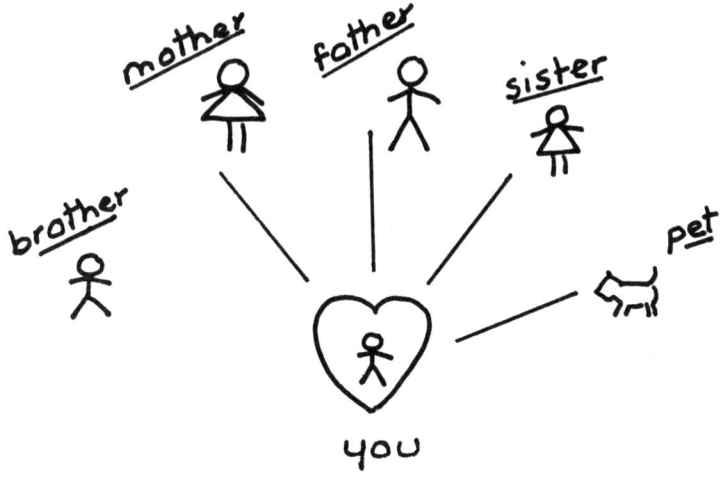

God loves you much more because God *is* love. His love for you is ENORMOUS, and it goes on FOREVER. You're <u>very</u> important to Him, and you really do matter.

So_ He doesn't want you to go around this way_

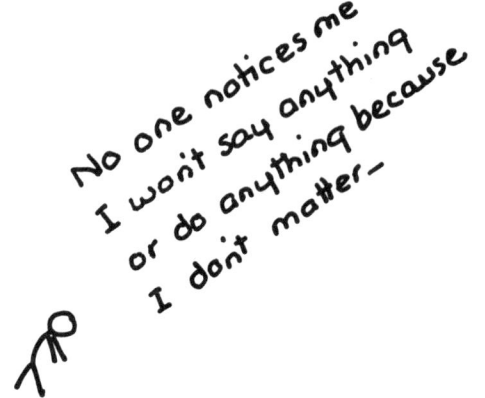

That's like a car that goes like this_

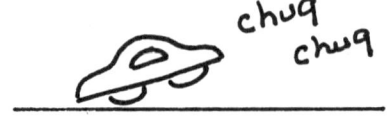

because the engine isn't working well.

God wants you to go around this way-

That's like a car that goes like this—

because the engine's running

25

well, and it's doing everything that it was designed to do.

Does God love some people more than others?

No. He loves everyone just the same, whether they're:

rich　　　　or　　　　poor

strong　　　or　　　　weak

healthy　　　or　　　　sick

smart　or　not　very　smart

good looking   or   not very
                    good looking

And He loves us no matter:

      what we do

      how we do it

      where we go

      what we say

He loves us when we're good —
                           ☺

and He loves us when we're bad —
                             ☹

BUT —

He doesn't love the bad things

that we might do.

AND_
He wants us to love Him as He loves us.

How far can God's love reach?

While God is loving you right now, do you suppose that there's enough love left over to love all these other people who are:

skating in Holland

skiing in Switzerland

swimming in Australia

riding in England

water skiing in America

?

Yes, there's enough love everywhere for everyone. God's love reaches all around the world.

And God's love never comes to an end.

A car runs out of gas and the tank has to be filled up,

doesn't it? Well, there's <u>no end</u> to god's love for us.

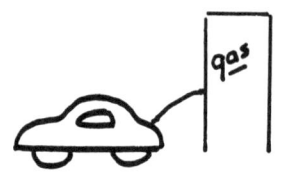

a car runs out of gas

BUT_

god never runs out of love.

How much does God know about me?

God knows so much about you that He knows the number of hairs that you have on your head. Do <u>you</u> know that number?

123?
368?
Hmmm—

592?
1784?
Hmmm—

Well then, if you don't know,

and if God <u>does</u>, that means that God knows you better than you know yourself.

And as a matter of fact, God tells us in the Bible that He even knows our thoughts before we think them. Yes, God sees the thoughts that we're going to think after the ones that we're thinking right now.

☺ I guess I'll —

God already knows

Maybe I'll —

god already knows

How long has God known about me?

God knew about you long before you were born. When He made the world, He knew all about you. And He planned you <u>exactly</u> as you are.

Is your hair
    black
    brown ?
    yellow
    red

Are your eyes
    blue
    brown ?
    gray
    green

Well, He wanted you <u>just that way</u>, and there isn't another you in all the world.

Do I _have_ to love God?

No, you don't. If you think about this, you'll see that love to be real has to have a "Yes" or a "No" to it.

Let's pretend that you have a new dog. Of course you want your dog to love you, but you can't make him love you. Yet, if you're —
>nice to him
>and pat him
>and feed him
>and love him

he <u>will</u> love you, won't he?

In other words, he doesn't

arrive at your house like this—

I love my new owner

But very soon after he arrives this happens—

I love my owner because he—

feeds me

DOG

cares for me

AND HE LOVES ME—

Well, it's the same way with the Lord God. As we get to know Him — through reading the Bible — we see how much He loves us, and then our love for Him grows

♡

and grows

♡

and grows

♡

Is God always with me?

Yes, God is always with you. And that means:

He's with you in the dark of night—

midnight

He's with you in the classroom—

He's with you in the school

bus_

He's with you in the supermarket_

He's with you on the playground_

Yes, god is <u>always</u> with you.

Is there anyone in the world who is good all the time?

No. Not one. For instance:

Let's pretend that you decide, "I'm going to be good all day today. I won't say or do one bad thing." Then, just to be sure of this, you decide to spend the day in a closet. In there you couldn't <u>do</u> anything, and there'd be no one to talk to, so surely you'd get the job done.

Here you go

But do you know that even there you won't be all good? Because what about your thoughts? They won't be good all day — in fact they'll probably get worse the longer you stay in there.

I certainly am good to stay in here all day —

You see, the fact that you

think you're good is a bad thought.

   So no one in all the world is always
        very
        very
        very
          good all the time.

Would I make God unhappy if I turned away from Him?

Yes, you would. Jesus told three stories to explain God's feelings about this.

The first story is about a little sheep. This sheep decides one day that he doesn't <u>have</u> to stay with all the other sheep and, after all, why should he follow his shepherd anyway?

"I'm bored with the rest of the sheep," thinks this particular one.
"Who needs a shepherd?

I can run my own life."

So off goes the little sheep. And for a while everything works out very well.

> The sun is warm.
> The sky is blue.
> And the grass is very
> tasty.

But then—

> It gets dark.
> It rains.
> It's cold.
> He's lonely and he's very

scared.

Where is his shepherd?
And where are all those other friendly sheep?

Now, while this has been happening, the shepherd has been counting his sheep. As soon as he finds that one is missing, he leaves all the others to go out to find that little lost one.

And when at last he finds him, he's very happy. He picks up that little sheep and hugs him and carries him all the way home.

Now this, said Jesus, is the same sort of happiness that God feels when one of us turns back to Him...

Then, here's the second story that Jesus told about God's feelings toward us.

This one is about a woman who loses a coin — or today

we might call it a dollar. Now, she already has other dollars, but that doesn't matter — she's worried about that one lost dollar.

> She sweeps —
> She vacuums —
> And she moves the
> furniture.

Finally she finds the dollar and when she does, she calls up all her friends and neighbors. She's very happy, and all her friends and neighbors are very happy too.

That's the way it is in heaven when one person who is lost to God, turns back to Him.

But now, that lost dollar is different from the lost sheep. The sheep, you see, went off on his own — he decided to leave. But the dollar couldn't think about it, could it? The dollar was dropped.

The sheep could do this:

I think I'll run away

but the dollar couldn't do this:

I'm leaving - it's too hot in that bag.

$1.00

There are some people who,

like that dollar, can't think it through. Yet God loves them too, and He's very unhappy when they're away from Him...

Then, this is the third story that Jesus told to show how much God cares for us.

It's about a father and his two sons. The younger of the two became bored with his life at home, and decided that it might be much more fun to go away.

So _"Father," he said, "please give me the money that you've saved for me, because I want to go away."

The father gave him the money and off went the boy.

At first he thought that it was all great fun. Because he was so rich, he made all sorts of new and exciting friends.

But then, things began to change. As the money went, so did all those party-friends, until finally the boy was left alone.

No money—
No friends—
No fun—
No parties.

What could he do?

He'd have to get a job.

But the only one that he could find was the job of feeding pigs.

One day, while standing in the garbage and shoveling it to the pigs, he became very homesick. He thought of the wonderful dinners in his father's house, where servants passed the food and he didn't even know <u>where</u> the garbage went.

Dinner at home.
Where does the garbage go?

"I'll go home!" cried the boy, throwing down the shovel and dodging the pigs as he ran out of the pen. Oh, how good it was to start for home again!

And while traveling along the way, he made plans.

He'd tell his father how sorry he was, and although he knew that he didn't deserve to join the family, perhaps he could work in the house as a servant.

But to his surprise, as he came in sight of the house, he saw his father running out to meet him.

You're home at last!

His father—
    <u>not</u> cross at him.
    <u>not</u> scolding him.
    <u>not</u> blaming him.
    but laughing and hugging him.
    and already planning a big party to celebrate his return.

So that's the way it is with God, our Father in heaven, said Jesus, when we turn back to Him.

But the story doesn't end there, because we still have that older brother to hear from.

He was furious about the party. He didn't think it was right to have all that fun when his brother had been so bad — while he, the older brother, had always been so good.

BUT—

We've already talked about the fact that it's not good to think that you're good. And we should never compare ourselves to others.

Not —

He's having more fun over there.

WHEE!

But —

I know that God's doing what's right for me, and I don't care what he's doing over there.

WHEE!

So both brothers were wrong, and yet the father loved them, and he wanted both of them at home with him.

And, Jesus said, in this same way God wants us to be close to Him. There's a special happiness in heaven when <u>one</u> <u>person</u> turns back to Him.

If there's a God, why does there have to be Jesus Christ? And why the Holy Spirit (which I don't understand anyway)?

Both Jesus Christ and God's Holy Spirit are as important to you as God is. It's like this:

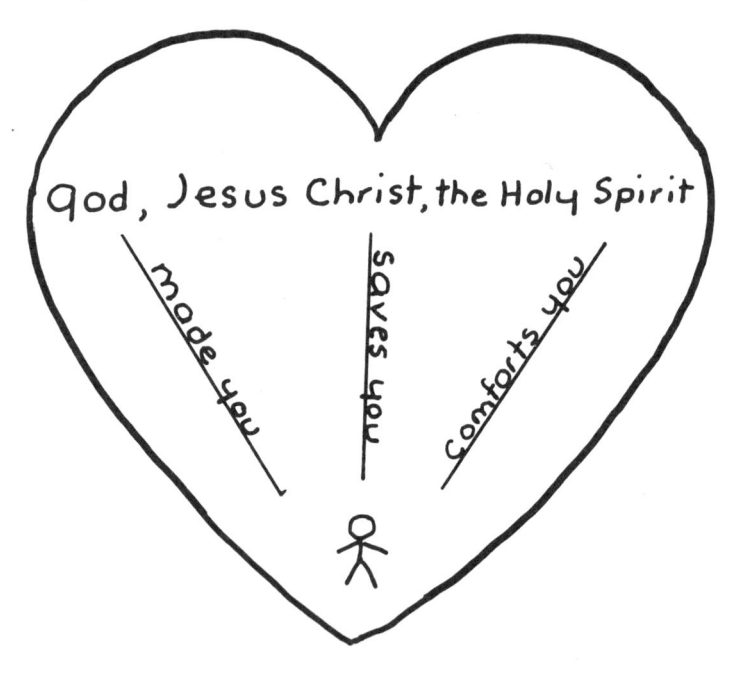

God, Jesus Christ, the Holy Spirit
- made you
- saves you
- comforts you

Now, you might ask — "What does that mean about saving and comforting?"

It means this:

As no one is good all the time, and as God is <u>perfectly</u> good, we're separated from Him by our wrong ways.

God
(who is perfect and pure)

S E P A R A T I O N
_____

      👥👥👥👥👥👥
us_
(not perfect and not pure)

There's just no way that we, on our own, can make ourselves perfectly good and break through that separation.

God
(who is perfect and pure)

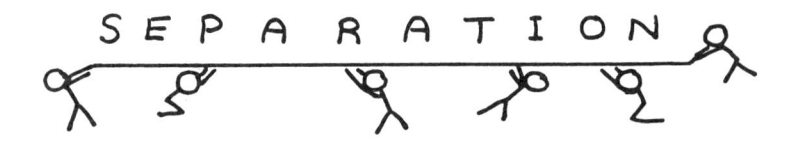

SEPARATION

us
(not perfect and not pure)

No amount of tugging and pulling will do it.

And whenever we make a big effort, this is what happens

😊 I'm going to be good.

😊 I'm going to be good.

😊 I'm going to— Oh-oh, here comes that bad thought again—

But God who loves us has broken down that separation for us. Only a person, perfect and pure, could do it — so God sent His Son, Jesus, to earth to save us.

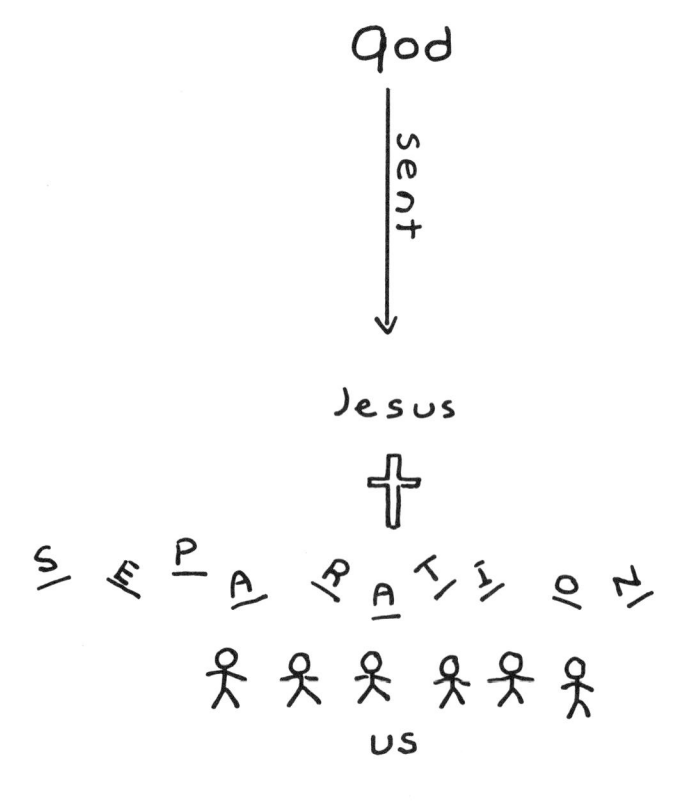

God
| sent
↓
Jesus
✝
S E P A R A T I O N
👤 👤 👤 👤 👤 👤
us

And when Jesus died on the cross, He took all the bad things of all the people on to Himself.

Now we don't really know <u>how</u>. We just know that it was a miracle and that it happened.

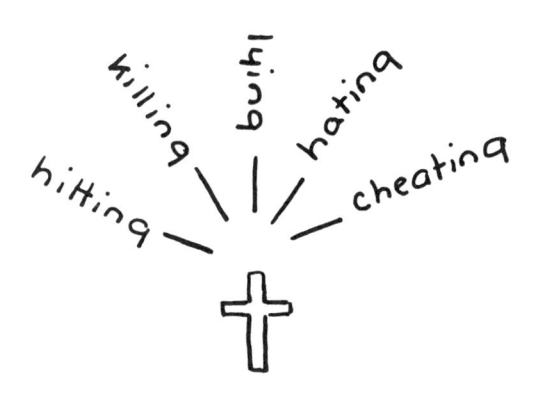

hitting killing lying hating cheating
✝

Then, three days after that,

many people saw Jesus alive again. He talked to His special friends, and later, forty days after the cross, He left to go back to God in heaven. But He had promised that He wouldn't leave His people without comfort — so here's what happened next:

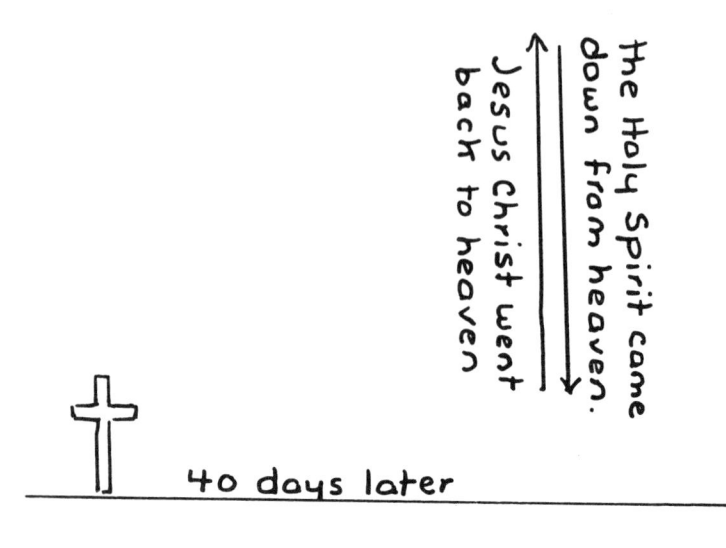

the Holy Spirit came down from heaven.
Jesus Christ went back to heaven

40 days later

Now, you know what it means to be comfortable.

Yes, but that's just comfortable on the <u>outside</u>. The Holy Spirit is here to make you comfortable on the <u>inside</u>. And this comfort is SO BIG that if you pray for it, the power is there to -

      quide you
      and
      lead you

and
protect you
 in every way
and
 in every part
  of your life.

But if you're wondering now to whom you should pray (god? Jesus Christ? God's Holy Spirit?) remember that when you pray to the Lord God, you're praying to all three — all hear you and all equally love and care for you.

How did it all begin?
Who made the world?

In the beginning god made all of the outer space, and every planet and star that is within that space. And He chose our sun and our world (which travels around the sun) for His special purpose.

*we go around the sun
here is*
SUN

our world
spinning
and
turning

Then, in His perfect timing He formed:

    our oceans and seas

    our dry lands

    and all our trees and flowers.

Then, still within His planned timing He made:

    certain animals that we no longer see today

and:

    the elephant with a trunk

    the zebra with stripes

    the leopard with spots

    the caterpillar with all those legs

    and the monkey that looks somewhat like us.

And then He made people.

Now there are two different ideas on the beginning of people.

One is that over a long, long period of time and after many, many changes —

people finally became _people_

The other idea is that there actually was a first man and there actually was a first woman, and that God made them both at a certain time and in a certain place.

But the point to remember whenever you think about all this is that God says:

"My thoughts are higher than your thoughts"

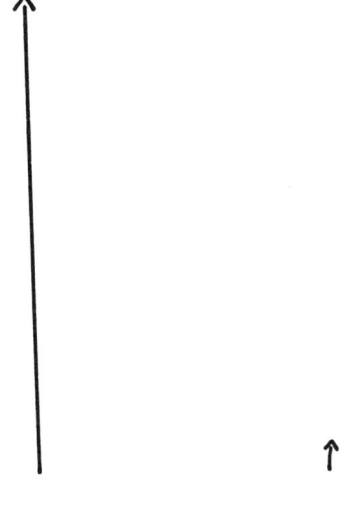

↑

↑
God's thoughts - our thoughts

So it might be a good idea to look at the whole thing in this way:

I can't figure it all out, but I do believe that the Lord God Almighty started people in His own perfect way.

and I think I'll just drop the subject there.

drop

When?

What?   How?

thud   plunk   plop

If God made the world,
who made God?

In other words:

Is there a god behind the god who made the world?

Is it like this.

a god —who made→ a god —who made→ a god

—who made→ a god —who made→ ◯

the world?

In the Bible we're told that there was no beginning

to God. The very first words in the Bible are:

"In the beginning God—"

So, you see, there was no before God, because God was always there.

Everything in all the world has a starting point.

people

cats

birds

dogs

trees

fish

Only God has no starting point at all.

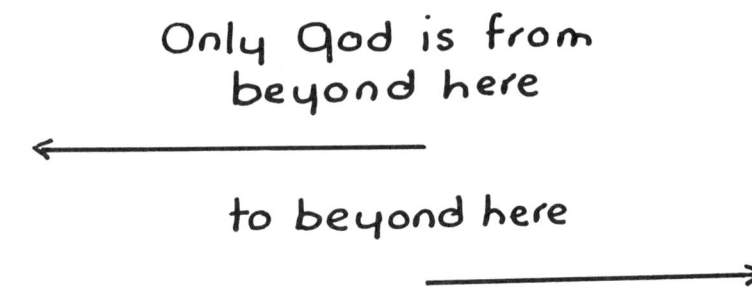

Only God is from beyond here

←——————————

to beyond here

——————————→

There's no beginning and no ending to God.

Why did God make people?

When God had made everything in the world it was all very beautiful and new, and God was very pleased.

(
a
new
clean
beautiful
world
)

with God, the creator - very pleased

But_
He hadn't yet made a person. Now why do you think

that God wanted people? Wasn't it all just fine without people?

　　Why men and women?
　　Why boys and girls?

Well, the reason is that He wanted us to love Him, and to know Him, and to be with Him.

The Bible tells us that God cares for everything — even for the smallest baby sparrow that might get a little dizzy some day and tumble out of its nice warm nest.

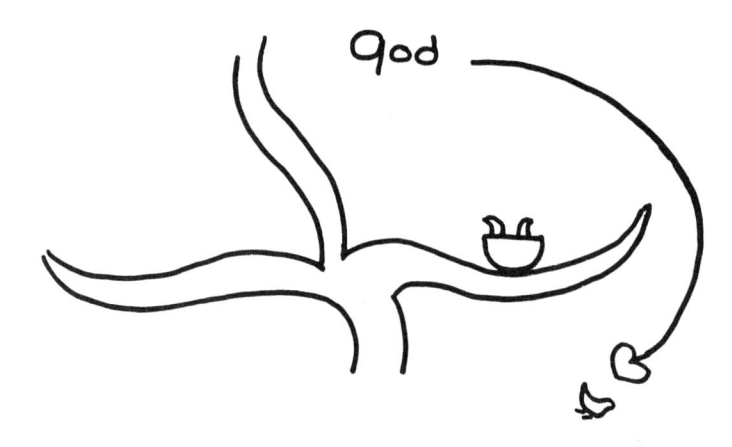

Then too, the Bible tells us that God cares for "the cattle upon a thousand hills."

But—

He especially wanted to make people. And because He wanted us to be <u>like</u> Him, He gave us a spirit, that we might truly know Him and love Him.

Is there really a devil?

Once, a long time ago, before God made the world, there was an especially beautiful angel called Lucifer. The Bible tells us that this Lucifer became very proud of his beauty. And as he thought about himself, and about his beauty, he began to believe that he was much better than God. His thoughts went something like this:

Who needs God anyway?
I'm beautiful.
I'm smart.

I can run my own life.

But the Lord God is greater than any foolish angel. And so God sent Lucifer out of heaven.

Lucifer is usually called Satan or the devil, and he's now very busy here on earth. He'd like us to turn away from God, and to think, as he does, that we don't need God, and that we can run our own lives. As a matter of fact, the things that he'd like us to do often seem to be more fun than the things that we ought to do. For instance:

The chocolate chip cookies that you <u>can't</u> eat somehow always seem to be the best.

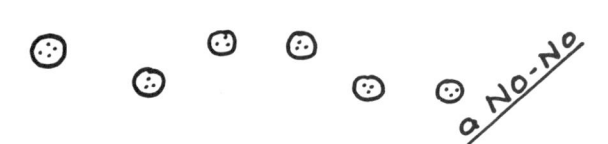

a No-No

The TV program that you <u>can't</u> stay up for always looks as though it's going to be the most exciting.

You see, the devil works in a very clever way. At first there's just a little thought way back here

That's not a bad idea —

It's hardly worth noticing. But then it grows bigger and bigger until it's a very large thought, and we're ready for action.

It's not a bad idea at all — I think I'll do it.

It all goes something like this:

It *looks* good

It *smells* good

Does it *taste* good?

It *does*

But that's wrong, and the person should have stopped when he was first tempted.

Yes, but how?

How can we stop a thought before it gets too big?

We must ask God to help us and to give us the strength to say

"NO!"

when we first notice that bad thought cooking somewhere in the back of our heads.

Why did god make the devil?

You weren't born with a tag on you saying-

I love God

No_

You came into the world with a choice _ to love God or not to love Him. And if a person chooses <u>not</u> to love Him, what's at the end of that choice _

the one opposite god

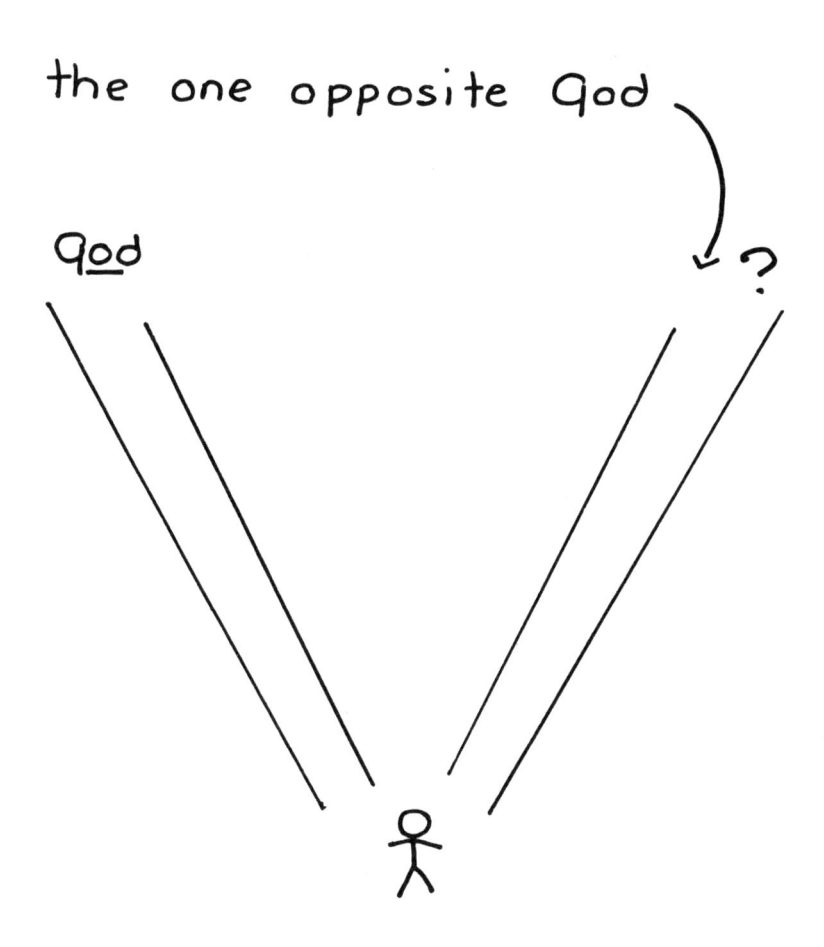

god   ?

There has to be something there. And god can't be at both ends because then there'd be no real choice.

So God has allowed the devil to be there — which means that turning away from God is turning to the devil.

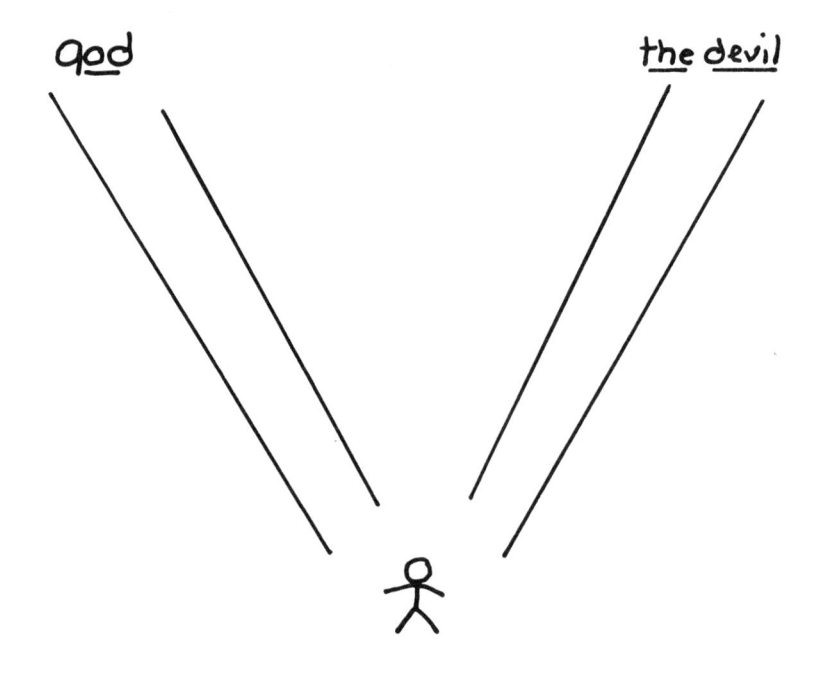

Then too, the Bible tells us that there's no way that we can stick in the middle between those two choices. We can't do this:

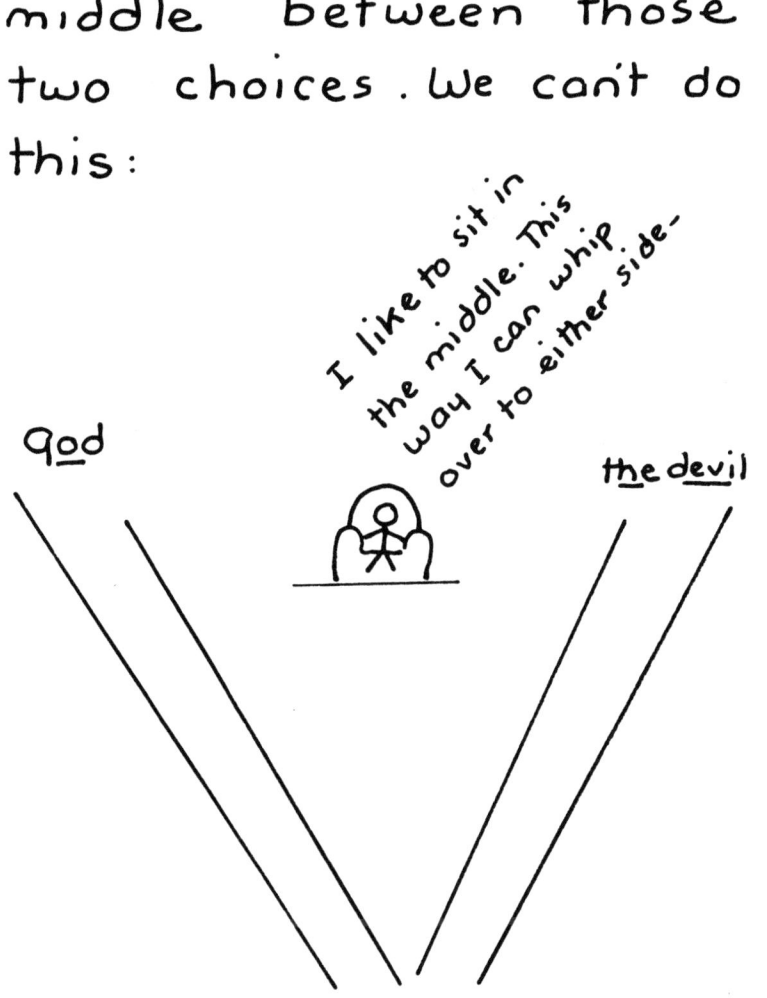

I like to sit in the middle. This way I can whip over to either side-

god / \ the devil

No — we have to make a choice — either we turn to God or we don't. The devil is there to tempt us, but the Lord God is there too — wanting us to choose Him so that He can show us His love and how much He cares for us.

Does the Bible have a happy ending?

Have you read any of those stories that end like this:

And they lived happily ever after ?

Well, the Bible ends that way too. But then, unlike some of those stories, the Bible has a happy <u>beginning</u> too.

Now what went wrong between that happy beginning and that happy ending?

happiness 😊   what's going on here ?   happiness 😊

beginning   ending

Unfortunately, the devil got into the act. You see, God planned a perfect world in which people were to be happy and to enjoy life forever. He made a beautiful garden which He called Eden. He gave Eden to the first man into whom He breathed a living spirit, whose name was Adam - and to Adam's wife, whose name was Eve.

They could enjoy it forever and they could live so close to God, the Bible says, that they could walk with Him in the cool of the evening.

It was perfect -
It was like heaven.

There was just the fruit of one tree among all the trees of Eden that Adam and Eve should not eat, said God.

But — that was when the devil decided to make his move.

"Why not eat it?" he whispered to Eve. God doesn't really mean what He says. Who needs God anyway? You can run your own life."

god said "DO NOT EAT It"

the devil said It'll be much more fun if you do.

Now, the fruit itself wasn't evil. The point was that by eating it, Adam and Eve would be doing just what God had told them not to do. If they ate it they would then know what it is to be bad — they would then have experienced evil.

It was as though God had said:

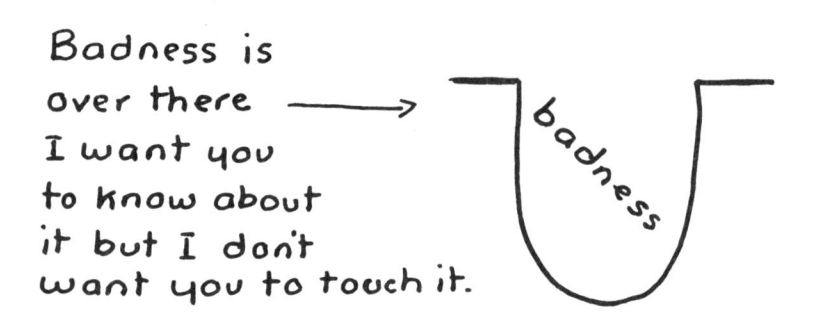

Badness is over there ⟶
I want you to know about it but I don't want you to touch it.

badness

BUT—

they wanted to go over there and see for themselves.

AND—

in no time at all, there they were in the middle of it.

Yes, Adam and Eve ate the fruit. And it wasn't all that good, as they soon found out, because:

God <u>did</u> mean what He had said.
They <u>did</u> need God
And they <u>couldn't</u> run their own lives.

At that point, all that had been perfect changed and was no longer perfect. There were:

changes in the weather

thunder storms and lightning

changes in the land

weeds and poison ivy

changes in people and animals

headaches and   sore
stomach aches   feet

Gone was Eden
Gone was that perfect life
     that was to last forever.
and.
Gone were those walks with
God in the cool of the evening.

But God is always loving and caring, and even after that big problem in Eden, He didn't turn away from Adam and Eve. He promised way back then to send His Son, Jesus Christ, to save the people — and later on, to send His Son again — to get rid of the devil and to make the world perfect.

And what could be a happier ending than that?

I'd like to be happy and safe forever. How do I go about it?

Jesus says, "I stand at the door and knock..." and that means that He's knocking at the door of your heart.

BUT_

He won't come in unless you invite Him in. Let's pretend that it's like this_

There's only one knob

on that door, and it's on the inside. You see, <u>you</u> have to open the door and invite Him in.

So there's an "If" to all this.

> <u>If</u> you open the door you can be happy and safe forever.

Yes, but you may be planning now to ask Jesus into

just a small part of your life.

BUT YOU CAN'T

Jesus says that's just as though you were to try to make an old pair of pants into a new one by sewing on some patches. You wouldn't then have a <u>new</u> pair of pants, you'd have a patched-up <u>old</u> pair.

He wants to come into your life and give you

a whole new life.

Not this:

old blue jeans, patched up

but this:

new blue jeans

Not this:

☺

old life with a
few new ways

but this:

☺

new life with
all new ways

So, you see, it's no good to say, for instance:

> I'll let Jesus into my life on Sunday, but during the week I'll take over myself. And as for Saturday - it's the best day of my week

and I know that I
can do a better job
with it than He can.

But that's wrong thinking.
Your week shouldn't look
like this.

Sun. JESUS	Mon. me	Tues. me	Wed. me
Thurs. me	Fri. me	Sat. ME	

It should look like this.

Sun.	Mon.	Tues.	Wed.
Thurs.	Fri.	Sat.	

JESUS (written across the table)

And if you do let Jesus take over your whole week (and month and year and life) you'll find that your days go along much more smoothly, and that your Saturdays are

    MUCH
    MORE
    FUN.

What is heaven like?

There are lots of things about heaven that we don't know — but there are certain things that we do know, because God has told us about them in the Bible. Here are some of them:

God and Jesus Christ and God's Holy Spirit are there covering all of heaven with love and happiness and joy.

Heaven is more fun than <u>anything</u> we've <u>ever</u> done (or even thought about) here on earth.

better than going to parties.

better than eating ice cream.

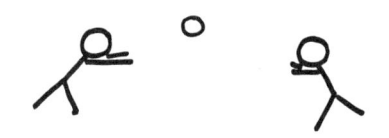

better than playing games.

There's no—
> sorrow
> or
> sadness
> or
> crying
>> in heaven.

There are no—
> headaches
> or
> sore throats
> or
> cuts and bruises
>> in heaven.

There's no—
> darkness
> or
> blackness
> or
> lost-ness
>> in heaven.

There's no-
    time
       in heaven.

Everyone is
      always
      and
      always
      and
      always
        in heaven.

And everyone is together
                forever.

:) Hello!   :) Hello!

  Yes, heaven is a promise from God for all those who love Him and who believe in Him. In other words, it isn't a promise just because, for instance —

> We sit in the front pew
> in Church each Sunday
>
> We're good quite a bit
> of the time
>
> We only lose our tempers
> when things get very bad

Heaven isn't even promised for those of us who might get around to learning the whole Bible by heart some day. No, it's there for those of us who love the Lord.

What does God want me to do if someone is mean to me?

Jesus tells us that if someone makes us go <u>one</u> mile
we should go with him
<u>two</u>.

——→   兔   ——→

1 mile   don't stop   keep on
          here   going

Now what does that mean?
A daily walk of two miles?

And what does it mean
when Jesus tells us that
if someone hits us on one

cheek, we're to turn around so that he can hit us on the <u>other</u> <u>one</u> too?

OUCH

we're to turn the other cheek

want to hit me on the other side? *Huh?*

Now, what does that mean?

Are two sore cheeks better than one sore cheek?

No —

The real meaning is that

we must always be nice to everyone. And if someone is mean to us, we must still be nice — we should never turn off that nice-ness. We can't do this.

I've been very good for most of the day so I'm turning it off at supper-time

☺

No — we can't do that. As a matter of fact, Jesus

wants us to be <u>so</u> nice that we even ask God to bless that person who's been mean to us.

And that word bless means to ask God for all good things for the person — like this:

God, please bless him with —

happiness

good health

good times

Not this:

I really don't like him so, god, please just bless him with—

:)

happiness but please don't over do it

health, but with some bad colds thrown in

a *few* good times but may they all end early

:(

Does god want me to be kind to everyone?

Yes, He does. He doesn't like this:

OUCH

He likes this:

That girl's hair could be pulled but I'm not going to do it

Sometimes it's very hard

to be kind to another person. Let's pretend that a boy is having trouble at school—no one likes him.

go away!

Now, what does god want <u>you</u> to do? He wants you to be kind to the boy who's in trouble, doesn't He? But in order to do that, you'd

have to leave the crowd —
and then the crowd might
make fun of you.

go away
both of you!

你   你   你 你
              you
你   你

But <u>god</u> wouldn't make
fun of you. He'd be very
pleased. And, as a matter
of fact, probably many in

the crowd would have this secret thought anyway:

I wish I could do that, but I'm scared to leave the crowd - I might be laughed at -

So we must always do what God wants us to do and never feel that we must stick with the crowd when we know that the crowd is wrong.

Here's a story that Jesus told about kindness and helping others.

A certain man was robbed and beaten, and then left on the side of a road. The poor man was bleeding and badly hurt, and as there were no policemen in those days, he had very little hope of getting help.

It was a lonely road with few travelers, so we can picture his relief when at lost someone appeared in the distance.

What wonderful luck, he thought when he saw that it was a priest. Surely a priest, a man of God, would help him.

But not so. That priest looked at him and walked right by.

Why?
We don't know.

Maybe the priest was late

for Church. Or maybe he was thinking about next Sunday's sermon. Perhaps he thought:

This is just one person—

>→○

while at Church I can reach so many people.

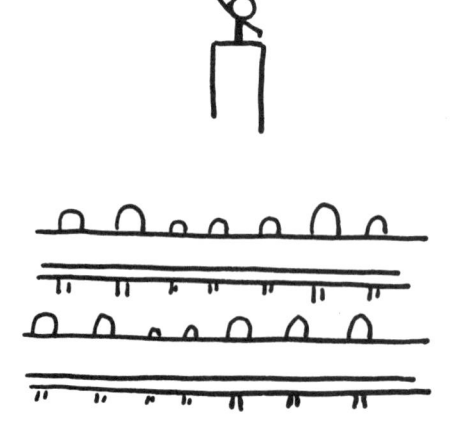

Anyway, whatever the

146

priest was thinking, it was the wrong thinking because he didn't stop to help.

The poor sick man was very sad. And yet, just as he was about to give up hope he saw someone else coming along the road. This time it was a Levite. We might describe the Levite as the one who passes the plate in Church. He also is known as a man of God.

Yes, but as this Levite took a look at the sick

man, he too walked by.

Why?
We don't know.

Maybe he didn't have time, although we know that he should have <u>taken</u> time.

But now, before we blame anyone, let's pretend this:

You're on your way to a party. You're all dressed up and you're thinking about the fun that you're going to have when you get there.

Then suddenly, as you're about to arrive at the party, you see a friend of yours lying by the side of the road.

you, on your way to the party

your friend

What should you do?

You can see that your friend needs help, but if

you stop, you'll miss—

    the games
    the presents
    the ice cream and cake
    and all that fun.

Then too, if some of your other friends happen to pass by, they might laugh at you.
    What to do?

    This?   or   This?

It isn't easy to decide, is it? Nor was it easy for that priest and that Levite. You see, they were just _not_ thinking about God at the time. Even a man of God has to be careful not to think people-thoughts rather than God-thoughts.

People-thoughts are: I won't help because —

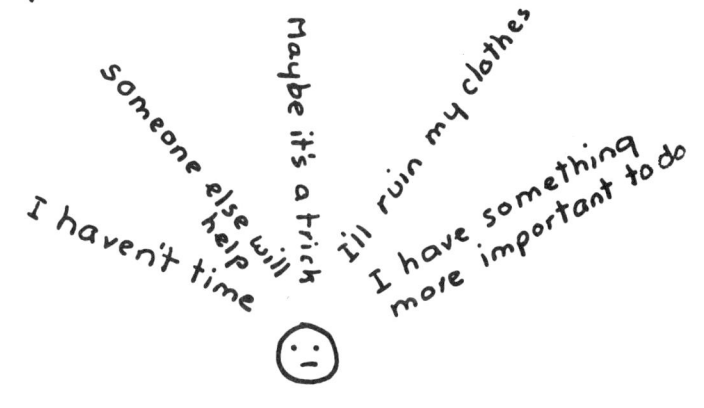

- I haven't time
- someone else will help
- maybe it's a trick
- I'll ruin my clothes
- I have something more important to do

☹

God-thoughts are: I'll help even though —

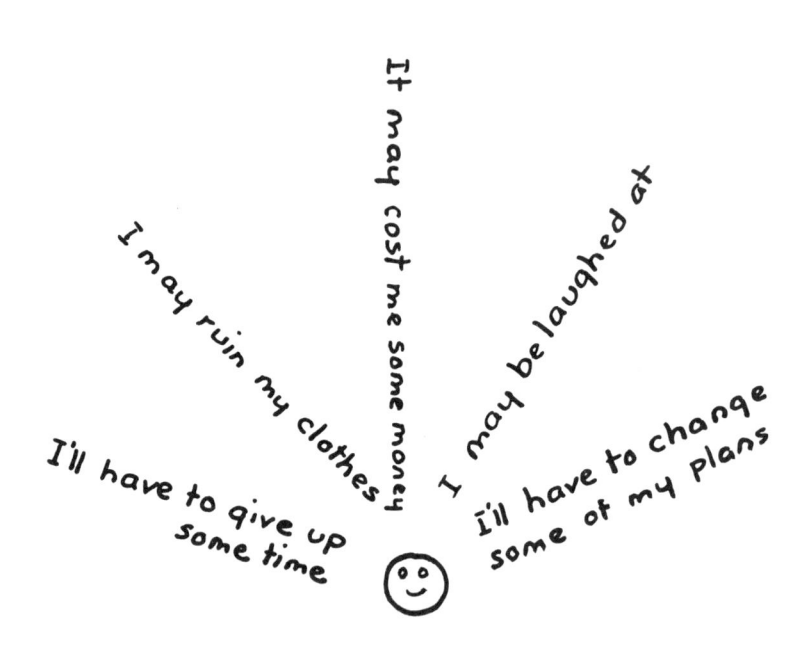

- I may ruin my clothes
- It may cost me some money
- I may be laughed at
- I'll have to give up some time
- I'll have to change some of my plans

Now, Jesus said there was one other person who passed by that day, but as this was a Samaritan, the sick man had no hope at all of being helped. You see, Samaritans were thought of as very <u>un</u>important people.

"<u>I</u> wouldn't help <u>him</u> if <u>he</u> were lying here," thought our man, and he looked the other way.

<u>He</u> wouldn't help <u>him</u> if things were the other way around.

But he was so wrong. That Samaritan stopped. He washed his cuts, he took him somewhere for further care, and he spent his own money to pay for that care, and for all the needed medicines.

And that's the way Jesus Christ wants <u>us</u> to behave _ He wants us to be "Good Samaritans."

When I know that I've done something wrong, what can I do about it?

When you do something wrong you must tell God that you're sorry, and ask Him to help you so that you won't do it again. Then, when you do this, God says that He —

    forgives

    and

    forgets

And the punishment for that wrong of yours goes to the cross of Jesus.

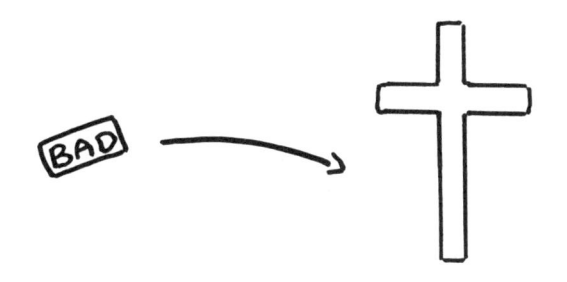

It's as far as the east is from the west, the Bible tells us. And in terms of outer space, that's forever and ever.

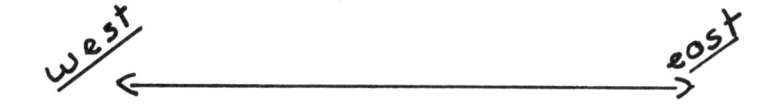

Then, after saying you're sorry, you should thank

God for His

forgiving
and
forgetting

And if <u>He</u> forgets all about it, then <u>you</u> should forget it too.

If God forgives me, do I have to forgive other people?

Yes you do.

You can't stay cross —

I'm cross and I'm going to stay that way ☹

You can't hold a grudge against anyone —

not even the smallest ones.

grudge *grudge*

You have to forget(<u>never ever</u> remember) that you had a grudge in the first place.

⟶ *grudge* ⟶

That's very hard to do,

isn't it? But if you ask God for help, you can do it.

How should I pray?

Praying is talking to God. When you talk to your friends, you don't plan what you'll say, nor do you always say the same thing.

Hi, how are you?

you   friend

Hi, how are you?

you   friend

Well then, don't always say the same thing to God. Talk to Him about everything – about your very deepest thoughts.

And remember too that you don't have to wait for a certain time of day before talking to God. For instance –

When your friend speaks to you, you don't think to yourself, "I'm not going to answer because it isn't the right time of day."

So then, don't wait for bed-time to talk to God. Speak to Him at any time and at all times.

Then too, you should listen to God — you shouldn't do all the talking.

Now, we listen to God by reading the Bible. If, in the morning, you read some verses in the Bible, you'll find that your day won't be like this:

what now?
which way?
where to?
when to?

🙂

It will be like this:

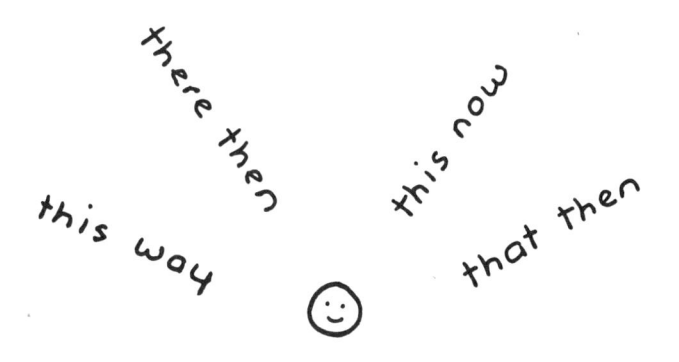

there then
this now
this way
that then

🙂

The Bible is somewhat like

a lot of letters to you from god.

You don't leave your mail unopened, do you? Well then, open your letters from God.

Will god answer my prayers?

Here's what Jesus says about god's answer to prayer.

If a child asks his father for a piece of bread, the father certainly wouldn't give him a stone.

May I have a peanut butter and jelly sandwich?

the father wouldn't do this:

Here's a stone

Or, Jesus says, if a child asks his father for a fish, the father certainly wouldn't give him a snake.

May I have a lobster dinner?

the father wouldn't do this:

Here's a snake

Or, Jesus says, if a child

asks his father for an egg,
the father certainly wouldn't
give him a bug.

May I have an egg, sunny side up?

the father wouldn't do this:

Here's a bug

Well, says Jesus, if a

father here on earth, who isn't perfect (because no one on earth is perfect) knows how to give good things to his child (and doesn't give him stones and snakes and bugs) how much more will our Father in heaven, Who is perfect, give us good things?

So now, when you pray to God, remember that you are His child, and that He is your heavenly Father. He is always ready to hear your prayers and

He isn't going to answer with_

    O stones

    or

    ∫ snakes

    or

    🐞 bugs

Are there some prayers that won't be answered?

Let's suppose that a girl is taking a test at school. She comes to this problem:

$$\begin{array}{r}5\\+5\\\hline\end{array}$$

and she writes this answer:

$$\begin{array}{r}5\\+5\\\hline 9\end{array}$$

She can't pray to god to make 9 the right answer, because the answer is always 10, and it can't be changed.

Or suppose a boy sticks his finger in the fire—

he can't pray to god not to burn his finger, because fire <u>does</u> burn.

god has set up certain laws, and these laws are for the good of everyone—

they can't be changed. So those sorts of prayers won't be answered.

If I pray for something to happen, and it does, did my prayers really make that thing happen?

Let's pretend that you pray for a good day. There's something that you have to do, so you don't want this.

You want this.

Then it all happens just as you'd prayed, which makes you wonder:

Would it have happened anyway?

The answer to that is that nothing takes place <u>by chance</u>, and that goes for weather too. Everything happens as God wishes it to happen. So God <u>does</u> hear your prayers, and He <u>will</u> answer _ but He'll always answer from <u>His</u> point of view which is far higher and broader than yours. We could look at it this way:

Suppose that a child prays—

Please, god, may I have an ice-cream cone tomorrow?

The next day— no ice-cream cone, but his father gives him five dollars. The child cries because he didn't get the ice-cream cone. He's so upset that he doesn't stop to see

that—

$5.00 buys

lots of ice-cream cones.

We should always look for God's answer, which might come out quite differently from the way that we expect it to. Yet it will always be a better answer because it will be given from God's perfect point of view.

What does God do if two people pray opposite prayers at the same time?

Let's pretend that two teams are playing baseball and the pitchers of both teams are praying this way—

Please, God, help me to win today

Please, God, help me to win today

What happens?
What does God do?

Well, first, we must always remember that we see our lives as though we're driving through a tunnel with just a very small view at the other end. God, on the other hand, has no such problem — He sees the all of us quite clearly.

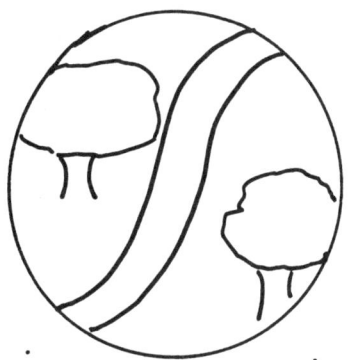

our view from a tunnel.

God's view — no tunnel.

In the Bible God promises us that He works everything out in the very best way for all those who truly love Him. So even though, from our tunnel-view some of the prayer-answers might seem like big "No"s, we must always trust Him and believe that there's really a huge "YES" hidden somewhere beyond our sight.

So— back now to those two pitchers — one of them is going to lose, but still—

if they both love God and have prayed honestly to Him, then both of their prayers will be honored by God. For the one who loses it will be like this:

From his tunnel-view, he had wanted to be—

(the winner!)

instead — this happened

the loser

But — all because God had a bigger plan. Now, that pitcher might never know the <u>what</u> or the <u>how</u> or the <u>why</u> of God's plan. But that's not the point. We shouldn't try to out-think God. We should simply say something like this —

I know that God has a <u>what</u> and <u>how</u> and a <u>why</u>. And because I know too that He made the world, and He hung the moon, I believe that He has answered my prayer in a way that I can't figure out just now.

And as for that losing pitcher — maybe God wanted Him to learn to <u>lose</u> before he could <u>win</u>.

To do this —

Congratulations — you played well!

instead of this—

I hate to lose!

Or maybe he was just a little too proud of his pitching—

I'm the world's best pitcher—

when his thoughts should have been.

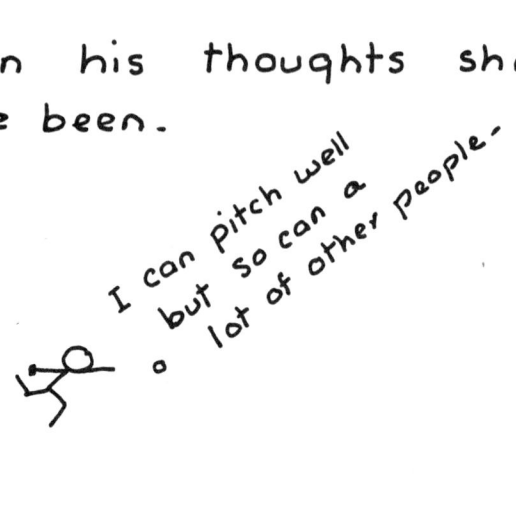

I can pitch well but so can a lot of other people—

God always has His reasons as He carries out His perfect plans.

Yet you might wonder now:

> If God is going to fix it up in His Own way, what's the point to my praying? Why waste the time?

Well, but God never promised that everything would work out for the best for those who <u>don't</u> love Him and who, therefore, <u>don't</u>

pray. He only made that promise for those who do love Him and who do pray.

So He always wants us to talk to Him, and to ask for His help_ and He's always there to give it.

If I pray for a sick person who's in the hospital, and he gets well, did the doctor make him well or did God?

God is behind the doctor helping him and guiding him — so your prayers for the sick person work in this way.

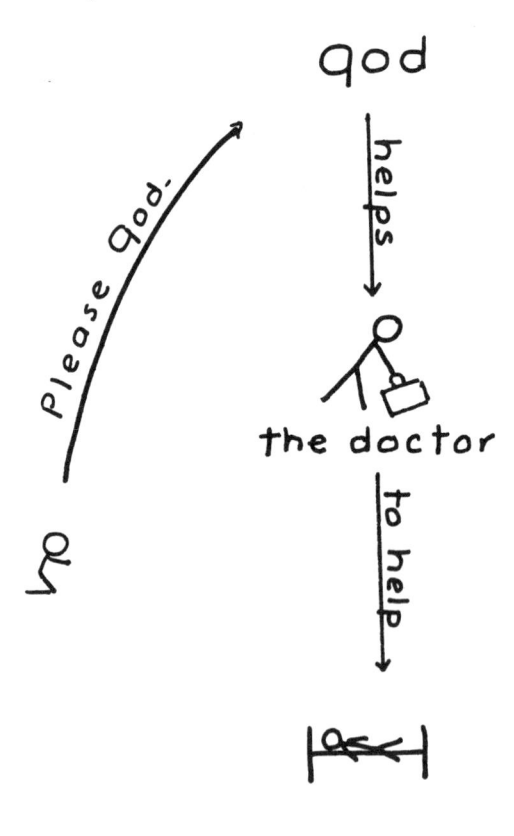

god

helps ↓

the doctor

to help ↓

the sick person

Please god ↗

But you might wonder now:

   What happens if I'm the <u>only one</u> praying- if, say, the sick person isn't praying and neither is the doctor?

   Well, that's not your problem.

   <u>Your</u> problem is <u>your</u> prayer.

You see, God will be listening to <u>you</u> anyway, and as the doctor has to decide

many things like—

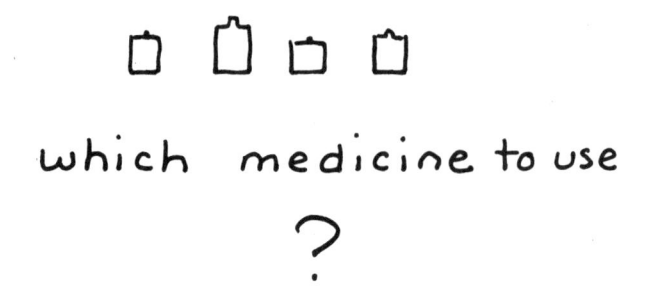

▢ ▢ ▢ ▢

which medicine to use

?

he <u>needs</u> your prayers.

Are my prayers really important?

Yes. Very. So don't stop — and if you've never started, start <u>now</u>.

And do you know that you can pray for people you don't know as well as for those whom you do know?

If you read this in the paper —

```
┌─────────┐
│  GIRL   │
│   IN    │
│ TROUBLE │
└─────────┘
```

PRAY FOR HER

Or if you read this in the paper—

[BOY LOST]

PRAY FOR HIM

You can pray too for people in countries where they aren't allowed to worship God.

Pray, perhaps, for some girl or boy of your own age over there — someone who may be going through an especially hard time today.

Who knows if there might not be some strangers in some far-away land who are praying just now for you?

And their prayer?

Well, maybe it's that you'll have all sorts of wonderful blessings.

In the Bible God tells us that if we truly trust

in Him, He will open the windows of heaven and pour out so many blessings that there just won't be room enough to hold them. Maybe we can picture that promise if we pretend that it looks like this.

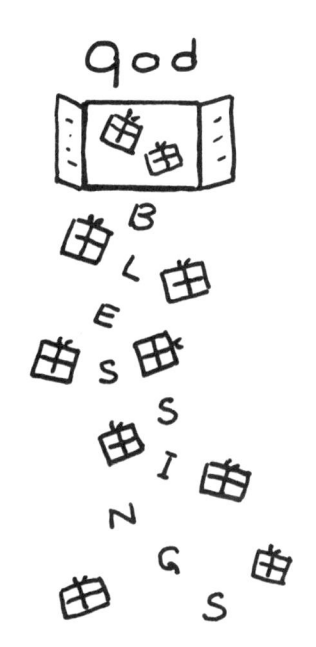

Prayers _are_ important.
And prayers for blessings are _very_ important.

And so —

As we come now to the end of all these questions and answers — you'll find a prayer for _you_ —

To our Lord God —

We thank You —

    for being You

    for making us

    for loving us

    for sending Your Son, Jesus Christ, to die for us.

And now —

May You please especially bless the reader of this book

with —

MILLIONS and MILLIONS

of

BLESSINGS

always and always

AMEN